CROSSCUT

POEMS

SEAN PRENTISS

UNIVERSITY OF NEW MEXICO PRESS | ALBUQUERQUE

Printed in the United States of America

ISBN 978-0-8263-6131-8 (paper)
ISBN 978-0-8263-6132-5 (e-book)

Library of Congress Control Number: 2019950683

All crew member names have been changed. Also, due to the number of work sites that a crew visits during a season, locations have been consolidated.

Cover illustration courtesy of Felicia Cedillos
Designed by Felicia Cedillos
Composed in Georgia 10/14

To the men and women of Yellow Crew. Back then, you were yetis. I pray you still are.

And to Sarah and Winter, for the many miles we will hike.

Do not go where the path may lead,
go instead where there is no path and leave a trail.

—RALPH WALDO EMERSON

Contents

III

IV

V

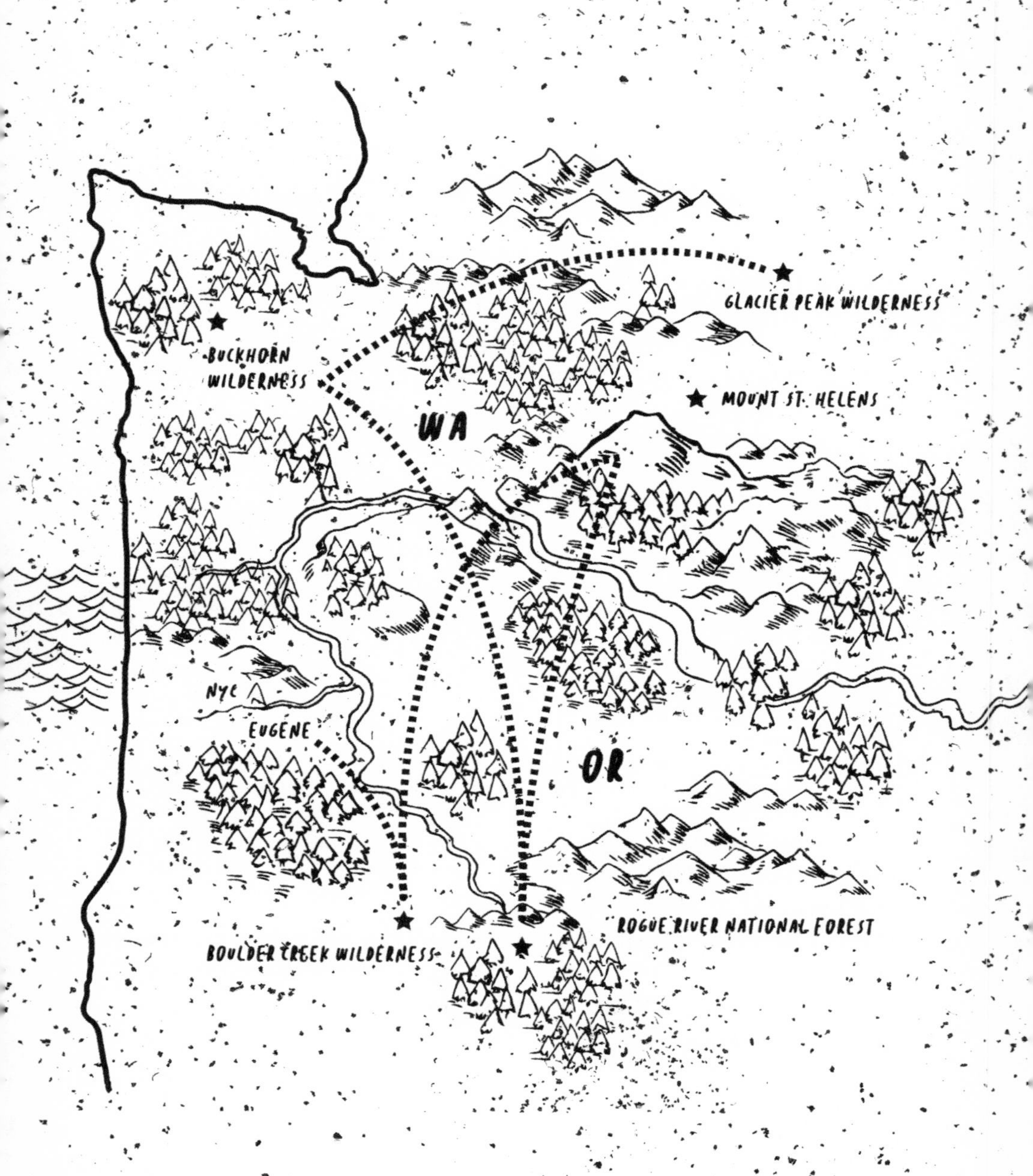
GLACIER PEAK WILDERNESS
BUCKHORN WILDERNESS
MOUNT ST. HELENS
WA
NYC
EUGENE
OR
ROGUE RIVER NATIONAL FOREST
BOULDER CREEK WILDERNESS

BALANCE POINT

I discover a Pulaski, a trail tool I haven't cradled in a dozen years, leaned under the eaves of this Civilian Conservation Corps cabin converted into a writing residency. I bear this cutting tool into a nearby meadow of quavering lilies and irises and find its balance point. At a dead and down, I raise the axe edge above my head and drive hips and shoulders into the swing, feeling metal sliver air before blade chaws into pine. Fists of bark and sapwood leap like spawning sockeye salmon surging upriver. I swing, again and again, showering this meadow in tree's rays, realizing so many things have changed these years but some things remain, though hidden, in our fibers of muscle. Remembering, and always ready.

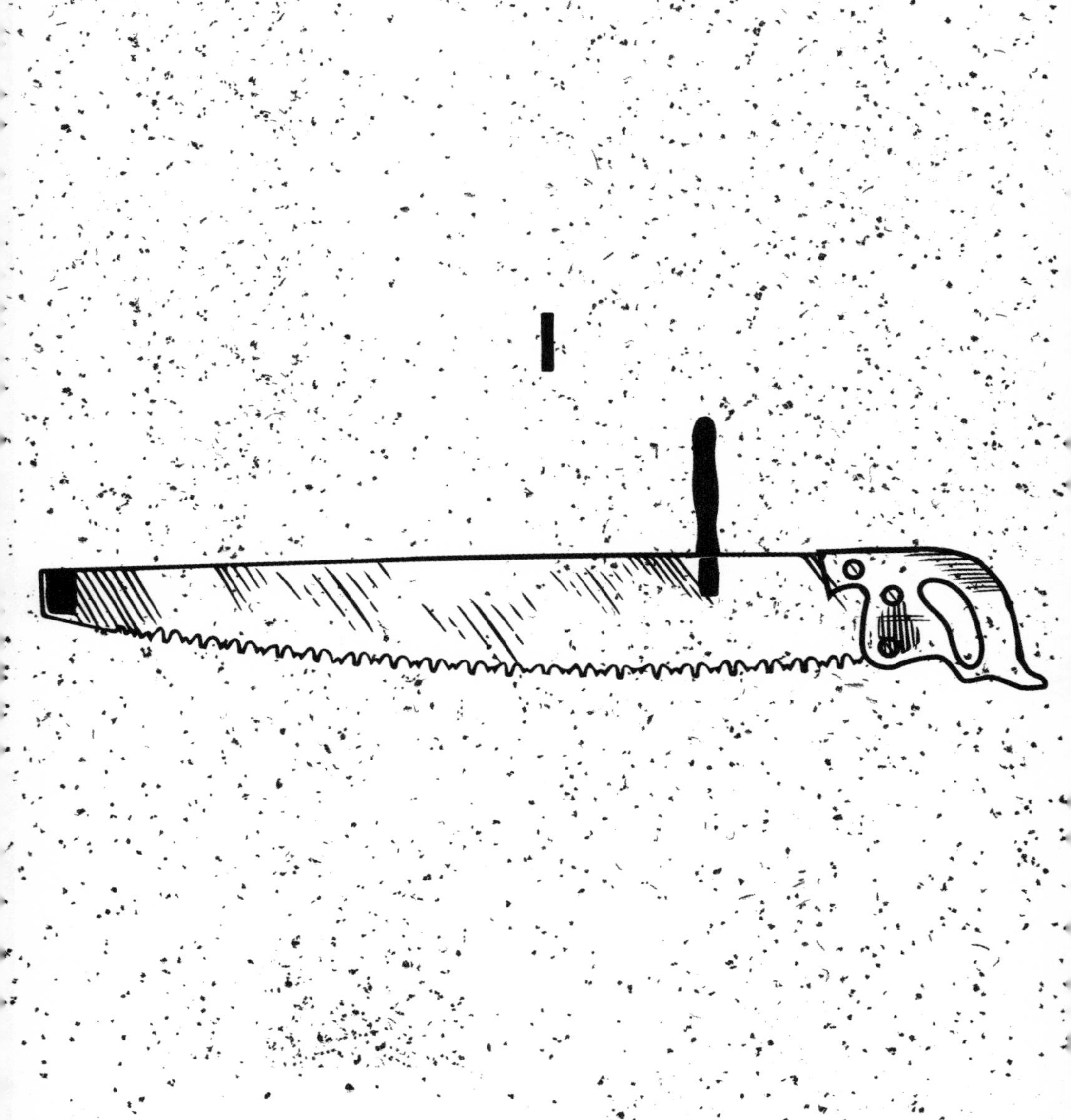

RETREAT

By twenty-six I have lived
in two countries & three states.
In an apartment, a cabin, a shed,
& a car—running & running.

The city where my lover lives is
an assemblage of noise, a factory
of waste, the racket of rush hour
noosing a knot within my chest.

I'm tired of temp work, washing
dishes, answering the phone:
Santa Fe Community College.
How may I direct your call?

Northwest Youth Corps claims
I'll get one hundred fifty tent nights.
I have never handled a trail tool.
I have only backpacked once.

I accept the moment the job is offered.

LOGGER BOOTS

Six days before I repair to the woods for a five-month
hitch, a salesman hefts over a pair of ten-inch-high
Westco boots with logger tongues & logger heels thick
as a burled fist of wood. *Two hundred dollars*, he says,
but these boots will be worth every dime on the trail.

I'll earn that cash in three days of building duffy
trails one Pulaski swing at a time or running a hot
Stihl chainsaw till my biceps & triceps scream louder
than the two-stroke engine could dream of whining.

But my feet, no matter the miles, & there will be
hundreds, will never complain. *I'll take them*, I say,
sliding city feet deep into new leather homes.

GOSPEL

These April nights, shivering inside white wall tents, we
echo the trail terms Woods Boss teaches us:

Angle of repose Angle of repose
Rock bar Rock bar
Check dam Check dam

These terms become hymns we sing during this week-long
Coastal Mountains training, learning to dig forest into trail.

Water bar Water bar Water bar
Hinge Hinge Hinge
Turnpike Turnpike Turnpike

We, future Northwest Youth Corps leaders, quiz each other
over what these terms mean in the forests of our lives.

Hazel hoe Hazel hoe Hazel hoe
Hog hoe Hog hoe Hog hoe
Cut bank Cut bank Cut bank

Woods Boss preaches, so it is our trail crew gospel.
Woods Boss preaches, so we preach back.

Pulaski Pulaski Pulaski
McLeod McLeod McLeod
Pick-adz Pick-adz Pick-adz

During sleep—hands instinctively curled as if still clutching
trail tools—we dream-mumble their names.

HITCH

This is the woods we're talking about, spike. Waking in tents, wearing a reek & grime that follows like a languid shadow. An April black-sky breakfast: fists of cereal followed by the grit & clump of powdered milk. A long hike—legs waking slower than our sluggishly ascending sun. By dawn, razoring trail out of tangled brush, a ribbon leading us deeper.

DISMEMBERMENT OF A STIHL CHAINSAW

Each sapped component—flywheel, sprocket cover, chain catcher—laid before us leaders-in-training: a dissection, directions without a road map, scattered seed from a flower. We study this orange saw as one studies a new lover, learn how this hard burl of engine misfires unless cared for like a child. These parts come alive: chain tensioner, gas/oil mixture, carburetor box, hex nuts, & clutch cover become organs, blood, lungs, joints, mechanical skin. *Dogs*, we purr, awed by sharp, biting pivots. Our round files pause on the one element that rips apart these forests. The chain, teeth sharpened, glistening.

WILD CACOPHONY

If there is a song during training, it is sung by the metrical pull
    of a crosscut bowing
itself through the pallid heart of wood, the heft of a hazel hoe
    dinging a chime
against rock, a mattock manning itself into the rock-ribbed earth,
    a Pulaski wounding
hardwood, sleeting brittle bark. It's like learning language
    through the song
of some new land, a song I attempt to hum each of these first
    training days,
a song sung by muscle arcing metal, metal cutting mineral soil,
    but I trip
over the chorus as each new tool joins this wild cacophony.

HITCH

This world is a genesis world unlike the rest we've lived
& we've lived plenty. None like this. Swinging tools
till muscles—muscles we never believed in—throb.
Fatigue rivering deeper than bone, an anvil roped
to our waist. Labor all day in the dirt & duff till the
bellow of *Tool count*, when we gather together our
wilderness of Pulaskis, McLeods, & crosscuts.

SLOGAN

The last morning of training, Woods Boss circles us
up to teach us the Northwest Youth Corps slogan.

Do the impossible, he growls.

We repeat quietly into a breaking sun.

Do it with nothing, he says, voice louder.

We repeat toward the dawning.

Woods Boss, smiling, caws, *Do it with style.*

We become ravens shattering into flight.

HITCH

After seven days we pack up white wall tents, break down stove, plunge sleeping bags into stuff sacks, van away from backwoods training toward, soon enough, our own crews & five months of projects. But not today. Today we erupt into town, find an RV park, rent $3.50 showers, step within hot rains, until, too soon, we realize it pipes this week's history away.

PAY PHONE

At a Mustang gas station stop, I find an empty
pay phone booth & call across our massive
continent to tell Catherine I've found a new world
bigger than anything I'd dreamt. *Like when you
found God*, I long to whisper. I long to tell her
I love her one final time, will call in three weeks,
early May, once logger boots next kiss concrete.
It is night at this Mustang, later night in her city.
Tonight I am drunk on summer, on fatigue,
on the task ahead. My hand strokes the coiled cord
as I listen to her phone ringing, unanswered.

II

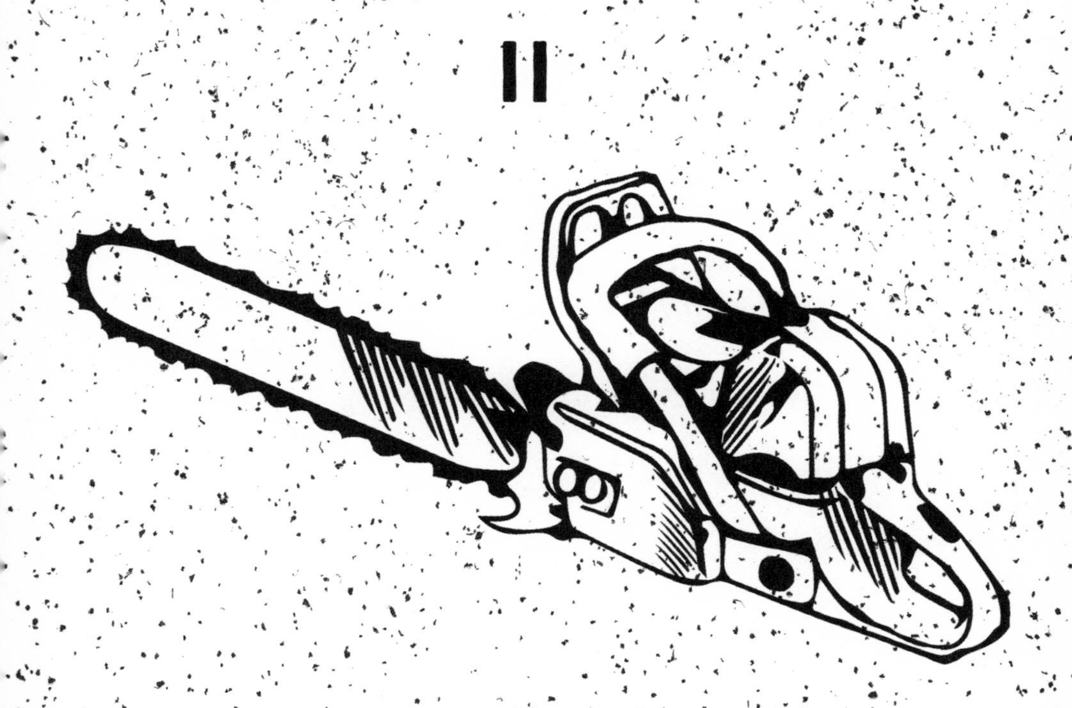

TRAIL CREW

Day one, I drive this new crew of teens south
on Oregon's I-5 toward the poison
oak–infested Cascade Range. Six teens,
paid hourly, slump in the row seats of our
shimmering white van. Apathetic faces gaze at
blurred firs as we abandon Eugene for
spring & summer in tents. When we return,
April flowers will be replaced by September
leaves. In the rearview, I scan faces, trying to
tease out histories. Today, I can only guess.
For a first time crew leader, it can't get
worse. Strings, a homeless heroin dabbler who
plays guitar like songbirds sing. Sirius,
hooked on pot & breaking into houses to get
money to smoke himself away. Red, a shy
red-haired McDonald's assistant manager,
one of only two women on our crew
along with Stacey, a meth addict who will be
here so few days we never know her myths.
Boone, recently out of alcohol rehab, wears wavy
black hair in a ponytail, like Shilo, except
Shilo sports a smiley-face wound ear to
Adam's apple to ear—a week old & scabbed;
someone tried to saw his head off. The seven
of us—today strangers—will spend months building
trails, returning to primitive. Today, tomorrow,
the five months ahead, I will learn this crew
the way rock learns erosion. Incrementally.

BEARD: DAY 1

Stubble blossoms
from cheeks,
a rain cloud shadowing.

BORN FROM EXPLOSIVE VOLCANIC EVENTS

We are embraced
our first three weeks
by nineteen thousand
acres of andesite
& basalt monoliths
phoenixing from
the western slope of
the southern Cascades.
Up a convolution
of logging roads we
drive till we terminate
at a sign that reads,
Boulder Creek Wilderness.
Here, we nest.

DAY 3 REVIEW

Strings is quiet, removed. Something bothers
him. Here or at home? He plays guitar,
then smokes cigarettes till he runs out.

Boone lops branches off trees like a yeti.
Converses naturally, nearly dominates,
then backs away so others can talk.

Stacey says I won't have a problem with her
work. I do. She sat down on the job today.
She questions her abilities. So do I.

Sirius reminds me of those tall kids trying
to hunch smaller. A goofy kid strutting
like some Portland gangster.

Red is passion for outdoors. Outspoken,
stronger voiced than even Boone.
Soft feet. Blistered. Works hard. She'll thrive.

Shilo lives on the Warm Spring Reservation.
Every time I look over, he's got a smirk
plastered on his face. Plus that pink scar.

Me? I'm wondering about how to
lead this gang of teens, how to guide them
through these wildernesses of our lives.

SIMPLE MATH

Day four, Stacey spits, *I quit,* sits down on the job. *After work we'll drive you,* I say, *to the bus station.* She waits just long enough for me to turn my back, then she's vapor or mist or breeze, wisping through Douglas fir.

We find her hitchhiking remote Umpqua Forest service roads, thumbing for wheels. I drive her to Roseburg, press a ticket into her hand, wish her well, wish I had another week to convince her of this spike life.

The drive back to Boulder Creek, Sirius asks, *What day is today?* Someone does the math: April 20. We hush as we each remember the last time we got messed up on booze or weed or heroin. Stacey's not the only one

running.

BEARD: DAY 7

Black whiskers begin,
like grass after rain,
to lie softly.

BOULDER CREEK

Close your eyes a moment, then
open them to that babbling creek
—what is its name? Maybe Boulder
Creek or Rattlesnake or some other
name so beautiful you long to hold
it in your mouth, run your tongue
across the sound, hush its name
back into the full-moon breeze.
Let the creek course its way toward
the North Umpqua River. This moment
I learn life is too big to hold. It is only
something to be tasted, a savoring.

MUSEUM OF HAND TOOLS

Nine hours after we start, Strings
bellows, *Tool count.* Everyone halts
in mid-swing & lays tools upon trail
as if in a museum of hand tools.
We count & re-count—
2 high-reach saws
3 handsaws
2 loppers
4 Pulaskis
2 pick-adzes
3 hazel hoes
2 hog hoes
1 rock bar
2 McLeods
1 crosscut saw
2 handles
—incanting names, ensuring
we've abandoned none in brush,
for these tools are nothing without
us, & we are even less without them.

BEARD: DAY 14

Cheeks & jaw
become a brooding
black cloud.

HICKORY

Seventeen days ago I bought
this starched shirt
at Hobi Logger Supply
in Roseburg for $20—one-fifth
a day's labor, but now
it is listless like morning fog, reeks
of chainsaw exhaust, Dutch-
oven dinners, mildew from cascades
of spring rain, earthen odors.
As I slide this hickory on
during another predawn bleating,
I consider maybe never
washing this ruined hickory.

DAY OF REST

At dusk, a first coyote serenades waning Venus
as she kisses these Cascade Mountains
before her early slumber.

Two ravens, the color of this eventide sky,
kraa to the faithful as if
for an evening prayer.

Today the crew is in someone else's
callused hands. No cloud of
dust from the trail of

McLeods, no members threatening to quit
before tool count. No shoulders
tight from the bulk

of the pick-adz. Instead, today, even
the Roosevelt elk bed down
in sun-dappled fields of yarrow.

TUMBLEWEED

After three weeks Boulder Creek
doesn't feel like—it is—home.
But our trails are built, brush lopped,
days done, so we break down
camp, cram it into van & drive
off toward laundry & shower
& some new home on some volcanic
mountain. We transform for
today into tumbleweed, blowing
up Oregon's I-5 corridor.

BEARD: DAY 21

This crew abandons your
civilized name, calls you,
Bull of the Woods.

THE BACKPACKS OF OUR LIVES

I

From a laundromat pay phone
in Cougar, Shilo hears
he doesn't have to return
to prison. He rarely speaks,
just scowls, but while
preparing for first
showers, he smiles,
I can stay.

Red hugs
him, arms wide as cedars.

II

During yesterday's break, Strings
talked about quitting.
There's something to be said
for airing our fears.
He added, *But my father . . .*
There's another thing to be said
for the things we cannot speak,
for the darknesses of night.

III

Boone's sister died
seven months ago. Three days
ago was her birthday. Boone
took
a long
walk
after
dinner.
When he returned he wasn't
crying. He told some corny
joke that made even Strings
laugh.

IV

Last night during dinner—
honey-baked ham
roasted in our Dutchie—
Red cried about
a lost lover. She wouldn't
say his name. Sirius joined in,
his own cries whispering
how he always fails.

V

They dream I'm some
put-together adult.
Catherine out there,
a ballast. But she's
on the wrong side
of unanswered
phone calls & I'm just
weeks since drinking
toward blackout,
mere miles from
the nearest store selling
Oly or Rainer in bottles.

VI

Once I dry off from today's
shower, now that Shilo
is off the phone, I'll call Catherine.
If she asks, *When does a group
become one? When does one life
become more important than
another?* I will say, *These exact
days, these peaceful nights*.

DRIVING LATE AT NIGHT, THE CREW ASLEEP, MANY MILES LEFT TO TRAVEL

In black silence I wonder what we are looking for—
knowing only that it is more than just mile marker
128, more than some lonely Forest Service road
alongside a river we don't yet know, all of it leading
to Mount St. Helens, to a trailhead where our van
will be the only vehicle, our crew the only voices.
This May night, pavement is broken only by our
headlights & the white stars of deer's eyes foraging
the low sides, looking for what, we don't know.

GEMINI

Once a symmetrical cone
till a lateral blast coughed
ash, tephra, pumice,
& molten mudflows from
a new crater cratering
Mount St. Helens National
Volcanic Monument. Now
a gemini: one flank eighteen
years later still bone-dry ash,
a latticework of dead
& down. The other flank, old-
growth silver firs, mountain
hemlocks, babbling creeks,
& duff damp with life.

DESOLATION NIGHTS

The small rise of Catherine's breasts, two snow drifts, a paleness found only in the gentle flakes of this May snow or the sad sight when I remove my hickory shirt & Dickie work pants before I fall toward sleep alone on Mount St. Helens's dark flank. In these shadowy hours, my head resting upon ancient volcano, Catherine's slender hips ripple across the tent walls of my mind. She's 2,918 miles east of this lone peak with its starrified sky above, big & beautiful but with so many stars that one cannot help but feel forever & impossibly alone. I'm desolate with nothing to caress, not even a pillow to wrap my arms around. Some nights I grow desperate for the touch of skin to remind me I am more than muscle, more than aching to bone.

STRIPPING

Week by week we grow toward a condensed language. Words disremembered, abandoned from tents & saw packs. What use for the word *sink*? When might we utter *closet* or *phone* or *bank account*? These words unneeded as a third thumb, unneeded as *money* or *credit card*. *Girlfriend* becomes little more than a weekend dream. After four weeks of woods living, I give you *TV*, I give you *movie theater* & *radio*. Do you want more words that these backwoods winds strip away? Take *traffic jam*. Take *fuel pump*. Take *9-to-5*. God, take *commuting*. Take *Howard Stern*. Take *pavement*. Take *concrete*. Take, we beg of you, *microwave* & *power lines*. Take *nightly news*. We give each & every one away because these industrial words taint our wild new memories.

RAIN GEAR

It hasn't stopped raining in thirty-six days, cascading water till Utnapishtim's ark would feel at home. All of May we've seen barely a wink of that sun we dream about in our tents, a sun to which we would lift our faces & sing if only it would shimmer through this St. Helens lodgepole forest. A sun we recall in hushed tones around campfires built from chainsaw gas. One of us, maybe Red, murmurs across smoky flames, *I want to see the sun just to remember what it looks like.*

Later we stream to our tents—let the rain snuff out our fire. In damp bags we toss & turn (the crew cocooned within yellow rainsuits) & wish no longer for dry hickory shirts & socks or even a home atop Gilgamesh's Mount Nimush. Instead we sleep to the song of our rain-river as it currents beneath tent walls, whistling damp melodies of mists & pommeling hails. This has become a life consisting entirely of rainstorms the color of lapis lazuli, soaking even our dreams.

NOUNS OF ASSEMBLY

If we were animals
of the forest, of
the sky, we would
become a drove of
oxen or a rake of
mules as Boone & Shilo
heft ninety-pound packs,
an unkindness
of ravens cawing
Lunch break, rattling
Tool count, bleating
Keep that tool swinging,
a cloud of gnats or a scourge
of mosquitos buzzing
about burnt rice, lack
of sleep, heat of day, rains
that last, honest to god,
six weeks, Stacey crying out,
weeks ago now, *I quit*, a gulp
of magpies as we titter
over some silly story Sirius
tells of Portland, a siege
of herons when we fall
silent, a colony of
beavers as Red & Shilo teeth
through firs & cedars
with a crosscut, a coyote
pack with Strings howling
songs of sadness as
a moon hovers above tents,
which might become
lodges or nests or dens
or lairs as we become
a drift of sheep with me
shepherding together
this crew, each so recently lost.

MORNING FREEDOM

On the tan flank of this mountain the Klickitat
call Loowit, the world is soft hues of dawn's
only breath. Beneath the shadow of our ruptured
peak, the crew leans into the earth & senses
a wild rumble, watches a dust-cloud twister
from mountain's flank. At this gray hour
St. Helens is dark with kindness; earth is only
ash. Soon a solitary Roosevelt elk—beautiful
in its tan hide—breaks from ash-fog. Then more,
forty elk appear as dust apparitions, race from
ash-shadows. Elk throttle this hillside because
they (as we do) love movement. This close,
we understand why they snort the way they do.
There is no freedom like this freedom.

LOVE SONG

Remember when I told you this crew had disremembered so many words? How we gave those words—*cable TV, desk, VCR, coffeemaker*—back to society, begged you to dispose of them? Just broken sound, glass in the mouth?

Forget all that.

For now, think of two months living in a tent. Weeks on spike without showers or shaving, days without changing hickory shirt or boxers, clothes faded to rags, stained of earth. Everything is conceived from rock & dirt anyway.

I need to talk about an aching.

Another crew leader—Ethan—& I spend a night in Hood River. Tonight we are human & in love with our women thousands of miles away. We also need something stronger than iodine-treated water, so we spelunk into a midday bar.

But I'm meandering.

I find a pay phone, slide quarters into its hard belly. Catherine's everything I am not. Pulsating lights, dance clubs, Marlboro Lights burned to the butt, hands of clay. Her voice huddled in a megalopolis of subway lines & tunnels.

Why is it so easy to talk to you, not her?

She fusses across phone lines about kissing lips not mine. I sever our line & stumble, not yet drunk, toward our bar. This June night Ethan teaches me last lessons of drinking to excess, waking in some $40 motel to an alcohol fog.

There was once possibility.

Come hazed morning no one loves me except the perfect balance of the Pulaski. I have no home except that echoing tent, that sleeping bag that no matter how tightly it sheaths this body never feels like arms, like thin lips.

This exact moment, I commit only to crew, to trails.

III

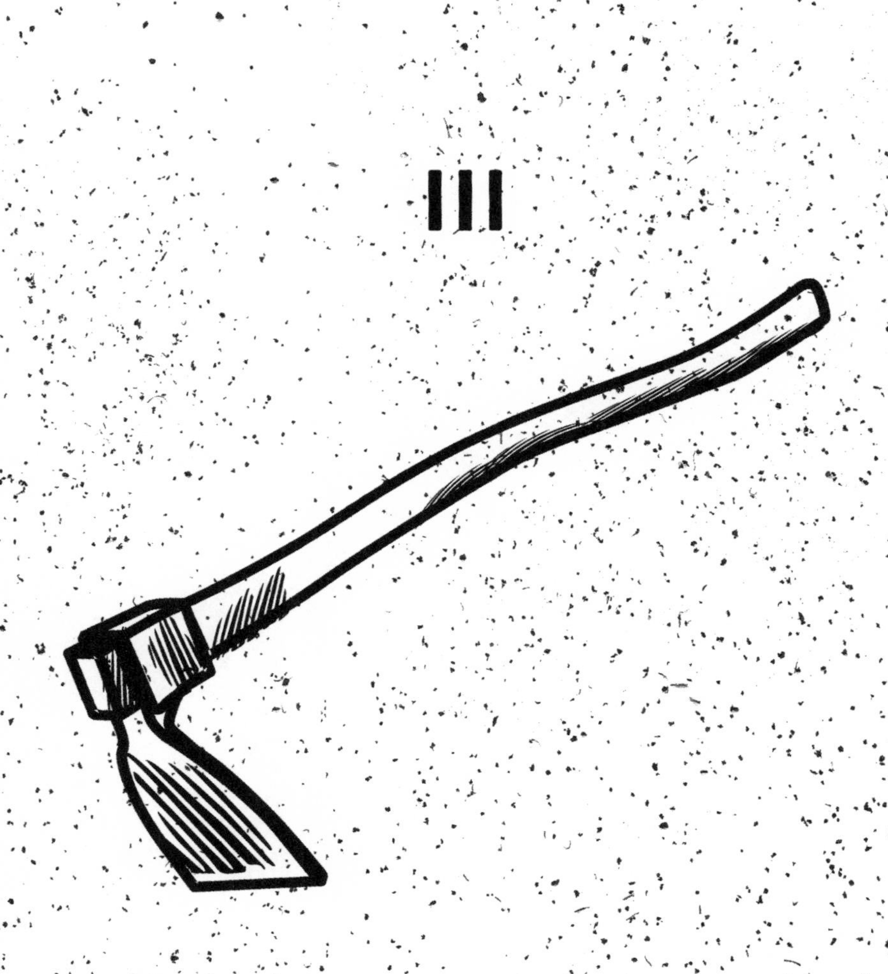

THE ROGUES

Inundated with rain that falls
as fog, showers, & sun showers,
as downpours & mist, rain that
evolves this June Rogue River
Nation Forest into emerald, moss,
pine, grass, fir, drab olive, cedar,
pea, or simply a forest littered
with Doug firs & Port Orford
cedars & the world's tallest
ponderosa. These giants grow
alongside hundreds of miles of
streams flowing into the Rogue
River, named for the Takelma,
who battled for their homelands
so ruggedly that French Canadian
fur trappers named them
Les Coquins, the Rogues.

RAIN ALONG WHISKEY CREEK

With skin wrapped around ash, fingers entwined around shaft, I raise the Pulaski & become more than myself—part human, part wilderness, feet rooted into soft Siskiyou soil. I arch my back, drive hips, swing this metal head till steel kisses log. Steady rain falls from that smear of gray. A steady rain of woodchips showers this trail. We bathe in dichotomy—wood & water, soil & forged metal.

IN THE DAYS AFTER OUR BREAKUP

A gray jay lands on the bending leader
    of a juvenile ponderosa pine.
        I turn & nearly say, *It bends, never breaks.*
    See? I am again surprised when you aren't there.

A weathered snag, gray & branchless, leans
    over the cliff ledge.
        I envision it snapping, falling
    to Whiskey Creek. I never whisper, *Our love.*

Small puffs of fog wisp with the breeze from
    the branches of a Douglas fir.
        I point to all the empty things,
    but you, like all the rest, are a ghost.

Another snag, spiraled tan, branchless, touches sky.
    That snag in ten years will still stand,
        will scrape only air,
    will scrape nothing.

A cedar harbors a kindness of bruise-blue ravens.
    I slow down, nearly say, *Shhh.* I forget
        you are not here. I wonder if
    the jay is still atop the ponderosa.

The ravens caw & caw from their pinion. I think
    about life's silences. Forgetting,
        I grab for your hand. Forgetting.
    A gray jay leaps from the bending leader of a pine.

THE TRAILS OF OUR LIVES

Sirius leans into a cedar,
bandana folded across scalp.
Mere months ago he was slithering
through windows, jiggering
doors, stealing TVs, buying weed.

My finger dances against
the flesh that presses against
the ribs encasing his heart.
Your heart is grander than
this cedar. Dream.

PROSPECT

Jobless loggers wearing weeks-old beards & aching
eyes that match mine sit at the wooden bar. The juke
sings Tanya Tucker. We each alone crack another
Rainier to get through.

Slouched beneath the marble eyes of dead deer, I dream
toward the darkest edge where Rogue whitecaps
sluice & batter suicidally before traveling to wherever
it is that rivers run, this time to the deceiving Pacific.

There is this world here within the Trophy Room,
another entire world out there. Under a canvas
of stars my crew murmurs through tent walls,
Good night. Drinking this fourth beer, I grow sick

for home.

THE TRAILS OF OUR LIVES

Boone bubbles up
an anger within, spits
venom at the crew
when frustrated.

Sitting in the dirt beside
him, I tell Boone, *Sometimes*
less is more, sometimes
others need a soft smile.

I babble all of this knowing
his anger & stint in rehab
are birthed from a sister's death.
Am I leader or psychologist?

PULL

Last night Red alcoholed this crosscut
    till it shone as it did
    in 1925, the year it was forged.
This July day we pull the teeth
    through a ponderosa
    slung across Whiskey Creek Trail.
Before, when it stood, we called this being
    tree, pine, snag, evergreen, totem.
Now, after it has fallen from lightning strike,
    we name it *dead & down.*
Red & I unsheathe this crosscut, set gleaming
    teeth upon a river of bark.
As the saw sinks into the cut, sapwood—
    callous thick—gunks every
    draw of the rakers across wood.
Russet shavings cascade to the Oregon duff
    as sinewy arms tug hardwood
    handles to chest, then loosen.
Red, ox strong after these three months,
    sways her hips & pulls, the eighty-
    year-old saw a quiet breeze.
Teeth sever cambium, sap oozes, raising
    vanilla—as if someone bakes down trail.
Rocking on the balls of logger boots, we pull—
    back & forth & back—teeth into pith.
An hour from first nibble, the rakers shed
    final blond curls from heartwood,
    phloem, underbark, & bark.
Our arms, even after hours, never tire of this pull.

THE TRAILS OF OUR LIVES

During her mid-season
review, I tell Red, *I don't*
offer praise unless
I mean it. She laughs, *I know*.

I should look at her
when I speak. I gaze, instead,
toward where I imagine
she might fly.

LOST LOVE

There is no world except this eleven-pound Stihl.
This singular cedar, lonely.
No firs, pines, spruces.
Just metallic dogs fulcruming a bite into a river of bark.
Cutters chawing periderm & pith.
A crack, a bark, a snap, a series of pops.
This cedar thunderclapping home to forest floor.

(Love? What does this word even mean?)

WHY AM I YELLING? I'LL TELL YOU WHY

I am yelling, Strings, because you're late every
freaking morning, because you left the bastard
file out last night & now it's rust. Because you
& Boone argue each night about how messy
your tent is rather than cleaning it the hell up.
Because Sirius burned last night's rice even after
I told him I could smell burn. Because I haven't
dreamed six hours of sleep in weeks. Because
my feet are trenched from working under rain
& in Whiskey Creek. Because my thumb is
a nob of undoctored pus. Because
I haven't kissed a girl in ninety-three days &
I haven't seen a girl I could kiss in twenty-six
& Catherine is kissing someone nameless.
Because my tent sleeps upon a bed of
granite, so the only thing I hold at night is rock.
Because I'm sick of being a leader, desperate
for one night at the Trophy Room Bar in Prospect
so we can complain about you, all of you. Since
I cannot tell any of you this, I commiserate only
with cedars, & they are miserable conversationalists.

HANDS & FINGERS

In summer's charcoal dawn, stir oatmeal on the two-burner.
Spoon brown-sugar-sweet oatmeal to chapped lips.

At work along Whiskey Creek, jam sore fingers into Oregon dirt.
Heave till the false cedar root snaps in your hands.

Wrap weary fingers around the Pulaski's curved handle.
Feel the steel head echo into manzanita bark.

Noon, ache back into the cut bank, a sandwich in dirty paws.
Cheap meat, commodity cheese, white bread, mineral soil.

Walk home in July heat, a chainsaw stinging shoulder.
Rest palm on the hot bar, feel the nibble of the cutters.

In camp, draw a bastard file across the Pulaski's blade.
Metal shavings turn into a shimmering mist, nearly a rain.

During dinner, count the cuts & scabs on each hand.
Six on the right, four on the left—two ooze pus, the rest scabbed.

In late evening, draw a round file through chainsaw teeth.
Nick your index finger on a newly glistening tooth.

Stick this finger—dirty from the workday—in your mouth.
Taste hot iron of blood—of woods life—upon your tongue.

THE TRAILS OF OUR LIVES

Gave Strings a verbal
warning for barely swinging
his tool, for snapping at Red.

He stares at the ground as if
he is worth nothing more than
dirt falling from an open palm.

Tell him, *We've built miles*
of trails from what others
consider mere dirt.

WHAT I LEARN ABOUT THE CITY DURING THE PAUSE BETWEEN DUSK & DARK

Evenings when the sliver moon is a bowl pouring out its first drink of constellations—Ursa Major, Ursa Minor, Cassiopeia—& darkness odysseys toward our lower horizon, I realize the thrumming & strobing of the city (where she braids her limbs within the limbs of another) holds nothing I desire (other than her) because within this darkness settling upon our society of tents, willows become silhouettes, a bat not yet driven to the edges of extinction hunts Whiskey Creek, a western screech owl settles upon a branch & caterwauls to this crew & the night & all the mice in this shadowy forest (warning *Beware*, hooting *Gather together*, cooing *Find home*).

ALPHA

Though named for Buckhorn
Mountain, which upsurges 6,988 feet
straight from the Strait of Juan de Fuca,
Buckhorn Wilderness is known
to those who camp in its lowlands for
the Gray Wolf River. An alpha
river that growls & howls so brutally
against boulders that strew its path
that a bridge built in the 1990s so high
as to preclude its destruction from
floods saw this torrenting cataract
snap its aquatic canines upon it, gnaw
the bridge into an omega, because
this wilderness is predatory-wild.

THE TRAILS OF OUR LIVES

Shilo whispers about a daughter
birthed from some one-night
stand, *I haven't met her yet.*
She lives in Connecticut.
He sputters *Connecticut* as if
it is a trail so long it meanders
beyond imagination.

I tell Shilo during his
mid-season review,
It's not just dropping
trees & repairing trail,
not just being beasts
of burdens. It's repairing
the trails of our lives.

AFTER A TEN-HOUR DAY

After ten hours swinging the heavy burden of the pick-
adz's steel spine,
my trapezius, deltoids, & pectoralis majors cry
a tired, lowly throbbing.
My abdominals, triceps brachii, & latissimus dorsi
quaver from time spent
drawing the crosscut, haling teeth through dead
& down western
hemlock. My gastrocnemius & soleus muscles
cramp & knot
from six miles hiking to Iron Mountain at dawn
then retreating
those feet-weary miles along Gray Wolf River
each afternoon. The workday now
done, I yawn into the deep embrace of this western
white pine's spine,
my head hushing against rivering bark, & move
not one muscle.

MUSIC OF THE WOODS

Red's axe knifes
        Thunk
a V-notch into a fir.

The sharp ring as Sirius's
        Ding
hazel hammers rock.

The sling of topsoil from
        Ssssss   *Ssssss*   *Ssssss*
Strings's hog hoe, a spray.

Shilo's grunt as he hefts a rock
        Kraaaaa
half as heavy as himself.

Boone & Strings jam a rock bar
        Ping   *Ping*
beneath a boulder.

I lift this Pulaski above my head, arc it
        Swosh
toward its calling.

ON THE TRAIL HOME

The sun sets from our measure of earth
as it does every evening.
Our Olympic sky drifts azure to black
as it does every night.
On the trail home we fall silent & watch
an August night-rise
birth our hushed world again, anew
& black & beautiful.

WILDERNESS LANGUAGE

Here on the peninsula we speak a language glued
together as much by sap gum as syntax, diagramed
with salt of dried sweat.
When we murmur, *Love*, I rarely think of Catherine;
instead I search for a sun dog.
When we say, *Pride*, Shilo rubs the rocks of his callouses,
passes a Pulaski to Boone.
When we warble, *Clock out*, Strings yodels, *Tool count*,
to the forest, then we stroll many miles home.
When we bellow, *Chores*, Sirius grinds a bastard file across
the cheek of an axe head, Red draws creek water,
Boone starts a fire & mixes Dutch-oven dough.
When we say, *Shower*, Red washes her face with waters
from the Gray Wolf River.
When we murmur, *Home*, others might hear mortgage,
electric bills, a fertilized lawn to cut.
When we murmur, *Home*, we see a gathering of tents,
communal meals beside the lick of flame.
When we say, *Home*, Shilo glances toward Iron Mountain,
strong against this Olympic evening.

SAVAGE QUITTING

The entire crew slumps between avalanche lilies & bell flowers, leans into cedar trunks, dead & downs, & boulders. Fatigue washes like thunderstorms crackling these eremitic Olympic Mountains, fingers claw-curled from rooting hands to wooden shafts, rooting into very earth, backs lock-kinked from slinging dirt dawn till tool count.

We draw cups & canteens to chapped lips that have drunk more dust & sun than water. Soon saturated, we root in our kitchen tent for food easiest to shovel in—pretzels, dry packets of hot chocolate, gorp, cheap cheese sandwiches—craving calories like I crave love, urgently.

This Gray Wolf River camp is, in these after-work hours, a current of fatigued silence till maybe Sirius mutters, *If I never touch another crosscut saw.* Someone else, probably Red, says, *Me too. Or a dang pair of loppers.* A third, maybe reticent Shilo, chimes in, *I wanna find me a freaking hot tub.* Boone adds between laughs, *A hot tub! Yeah. That's what I want.* Strings says, *Dang it. This is too much. I quit.*

Soon we all race to quit this handwork, sixteen weeks curled in tents, days drenched like wet dogs from spring rain or scorched under an August sun. Each of us shouting our notice till we are songbirds chirping the same melody:

I quit.   *I quit.*   *I quit.*

I quit.   *I quit.*   *I quit.*

Each crying what we want from that other world: *A burger! A slice of pizza! A hot shower! A river swim! A long night's sleep!* I almost whisper, *Catherine to hold.* Our quitting fills the air & steals, for a moment, our savage fatigue.

IV

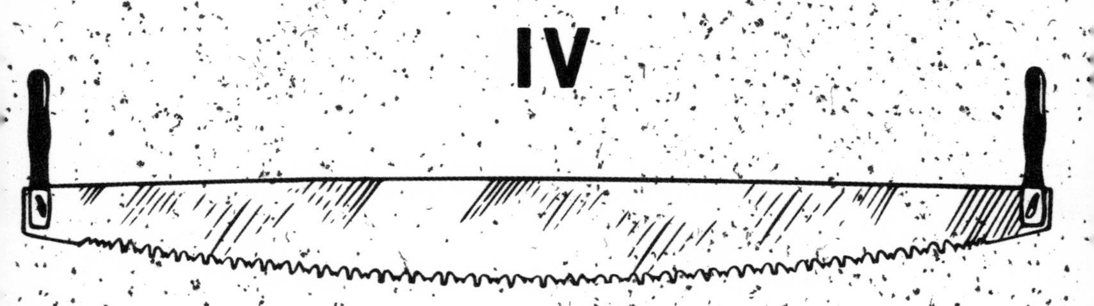

NOWHERE ROAD

In the rearview mirror I gaze at five worn
crew members dreaming into each other's
shoulders. Four moons ago I barely knew
their stories. Now I might be able to enter
their dreams: Strings to a soft bed in a house
with familial love; or to needles & lighters.
Red curling, questioning, into Strings, her eyes
flickering whenever I hit a pothole before
she dozes back toward a life spent in these
woods. Sirius leaning into a fisted hoody,
sleeping deeper than he has since his first
spark. Shilo & Boone slumping into their own
slumbers, carrying them to worlds darker
than this peninsula night. I scan the placid
faces of my almost-children as I night-drive
desolate Washington & adjust the dial to
some late-night AM station mooning country
songs. This crew seemingly so peaceful, I long
for more than three wilderness weeks till each
of us boomerangs to that next world, which
I fear might mirror our former worlds. Like
the singer on the AM, I croon a song to self,

> *Dear moon & stars, lonely Olympic*
> *Mountains, quiet Quilcene River,*
> *great expanse of Washington starry*
> *night, let us forever drive tonight's*
> *long & empty & black nowhere road.*

REMOTE

Mythed within the northern Cascades,
Glacier Peak Wilderness houses
more active glaciers than anywhere
in the Lower 48 & spawns creeks
like Agnes, which bruise banks
before plummeting over hundred-foot
bridal-veil waterfalls. Snow-crowned
peaks, tattered ridges, steep-walled
valleys blanketed, come winter,
in forty feet of snow. Not many
reach Glacier Peak Wilderness.
The best places are harder than most.
To arrive, a six-hour ferry up Lake
Chelan, past hills flaming from summer
drought, abandoned at the beyond-the-end-
of-the-road town of Stehekin, then
backpacks. Glacier Peak is hardest.

AUTUMN'S OUTFIT

These clothes were once wool of
        sheep, boll of cotton,
till sewing machines overlocked
        these fabrics together.
Workpants now aged into holes shined
        into knees by the kiss of dirt,
colored by rainbowed chainsaw oil
        & the dark cloud of gasoline.
This hickory tailored by rivulets of
        sweat. These garments wear
like fur upon the bull of the woods.

CONTRADICTION

Wilderness is a root that embraces
in ways no lover could.

To flirt with a girl, to dive-bar dance
her close to my chest.

No matter what time it is, it is the yawn
of daybreak. Forever.

An Oly or Rainier.
A long, sad bar tab.

An orange sun filtering
through Douglas firs.

Hours of escape only
Prospect (or her city) can provide.

This body sculpted
by mineral soil & rock.

The way shower water cascades
over a body, steals it all away.

By duff, by dead & downs, by wind,
by rain. By god by the rains.

BETWEEN

Night air
still as
a paused
breath.
Final
weeks
become
spaces
between
the beating
of a heart
& the next
beating.

ENOUGH

As night spreads its wings across our Glacier Peak sky, in my tent I untie the leather laces of these Westco loggers, yank gnarled boots off, & set them beside tent door, ready for cold dawn. Outside, as crew members canter toward sleep, I peel off hickory & double-kneed Dickies as a snake sheds skin. This bale of exhausted clothes I fold & set at the foot of my sleeping bag. Neither boots nor clothes smell worse than the other or me. Three days ago they cried for a laundering & I hungered for a shower of soap. Now we smell of earth, duff, cedar, beargrass. Naked, I snake into my bag & snap off my headlamp. The world evaporates into the black topography of celestial constellations mouthing upon us mere mortals stories of every damn thing I lean into during these quiet moments—valor, love, lust—but the only stories we have in this congregation of tents are of a crew taut like family, but tired. Still, tomorrow our sun will rise over the Cascades & the day will grow early-August warm. But before that first leak of dawn's light, I again will dress in my work outfit, again draw on knurled leather boots & ram elk-skin gloves into a back pocket. I will break into a dawn more shadow than light, more owl than stellar jay. Red, Strings, Boone, Shilo, Sirius, & I will assemble around a hush of breakfast. Like gentle deer we will walk, each mile closer to season's end, closer to this crew buckshotting into whatever darkness exists in that other world, the one of ATMs, traffic lights, & TVs selling everything under the sun. (Except for the peace of dusk, of dawn; they cannot sell us that. That can only be bought in sweat, in love.) For our remaining time, this quiet routine must be enough.

TRAIN TRACKS

A smelly tent is better than
homelessness, Strings says,
which is why I didn't quit.
Till just this week, our final,
I didn't tell these five that my
last home was a shed, my next
home a Ford Escort station
wagon parked beside growing
snowbanks in northern New
Mexico. Sirius chuckles as he
tells about train hopping
the wrong way after running
from rehab, ending up in
Spokane. Shilo, whittling a stick,
worries: *If I go home, I might*
shoot the guy. We see the scar,
a weary pink necklace. We trust
Shilo. Red sighs, *I need more*
than flipping burgers. For all
of us, that other world seems
to be train tracks headed east.

DISTANCE

I never wear my elk-skin gloves because I
want no distance between Glory Peak & me,
nothing separating these cracked fingernails
& scabbed fingers from loam, dirt, & duff,
no space between the heft of a hog hoe & my
calloused hands because the straight-grain
ash—polished by the sweat & oil of these
palms—transforms the hoe from mere tool
to an exact extension of my trail-weary arms.

TOMORROW

On the edge of this wilderness, two tracks
wend to pavement then to scattered
houses that bleed into subdivisions of
repetition that blossom into, just forty miles
from camp, Seattle, Everett, & Bellingham.
Sprawl so close to girdling us. A tangled
web metastasizing. Skyscrapers that fail
to imitate any mountains we love.

You can have it all.

ANOTHER KIND OF LIGHT

During dawn's first gasp, I search
toward where I should
glimpse ragged Cascades.

All I see are skeletal fingers breaking
from dark earth, returning
the sun its initial light.

Oh, to be a willow beating back
the bruise of night.

ENTROPY

Today, we realize this dawn walk is
        our last, mere hours of throwing
        soil, a final tool count, a final bastard
        file swept across a Pulaski's cheek;
        let the edge grow dull tomorrow.

TOOL COUNT

One last time, & loudest, String
herds us together so we can
chant our way through—

    1 high-reach saw
    1 handsaw
    1 lopper
    4 Pulaskis
    2 pick-adzes
    3 hazel hoes
    2 hog hoes
    2 McLeods
    1 crosscut saw
    2 handles

—the rest abandoned in the van,
except a hog hoe handle broken
during our time on the peninsula.
Moments ago these tools were
limbs. Now they lay inanimate,
wood & metal laid upon cut
bank. Is a tool less beautiful
if it is not dug with, not swung?

THESE DIMINISHING MILES, I PRAISE

This Eureka tent for halting
three seasons of rain & snow,
these hickory shirts
wrapping me like prayers,
the only ones to touch me
since April. Dutch ovens offering
golden dinners. Tools growing
into—or out of—our bodies.
Boone & sobriety. Sirius
& that untamable
smile. Strings & his five
strings. Red, a sun's warmth.
Shilo's quietude. Stacey,
even you, for quitting, for
teaching family. My complaints,
fatigues, failures. Yes,
my failures. This community
of trees & creeks. The autumn
of these days. Ravens on
a branch. Ravens scattering
into flight. But, if I must,
then to trails. May these trails
birth you & me—us—into
some new home.

ENTROPY

After five months spent returning to
primitive, we remember there
is no truth except all things move
from balance to imbalance.

BECOMING ENKIDU, LOSING ENKIDU

After months constructing trails, digging society from our bones, this crew has transformed into Enkidu before he loved Shamhat, when he spoke the language of those who ate grass & drank from water holes. At our end I fear Enkidu's spirit deserts us. Each of us soon exiled as Enkidu was; too soon we return to the rule of ruining cities, no longer home beside bear & elk, no longer drinking from crystalline creeks.

I-5

Returning to Eugene.
    Dull tools.
    Ruined tents.
    Scabbed & scarred skin.
April, this van overflowed.
    Stories untold.
Today, we sag into windows.
    Into sleep.
    Into memories.
    Into what-comes-nexts.
Tires whirl pavement miles.
    Humming what this all means.
    But we're traveling too fast.
Gas pedal on the right, brake pedal on the left.
    To slam that left pedal.

ENTROPY

A long list of lasts & finals till we sling
no more dirt, till we birth no more
trail, till we climb from our van,
till we—known for so long only as
crew—become you & you & you

& me.

V

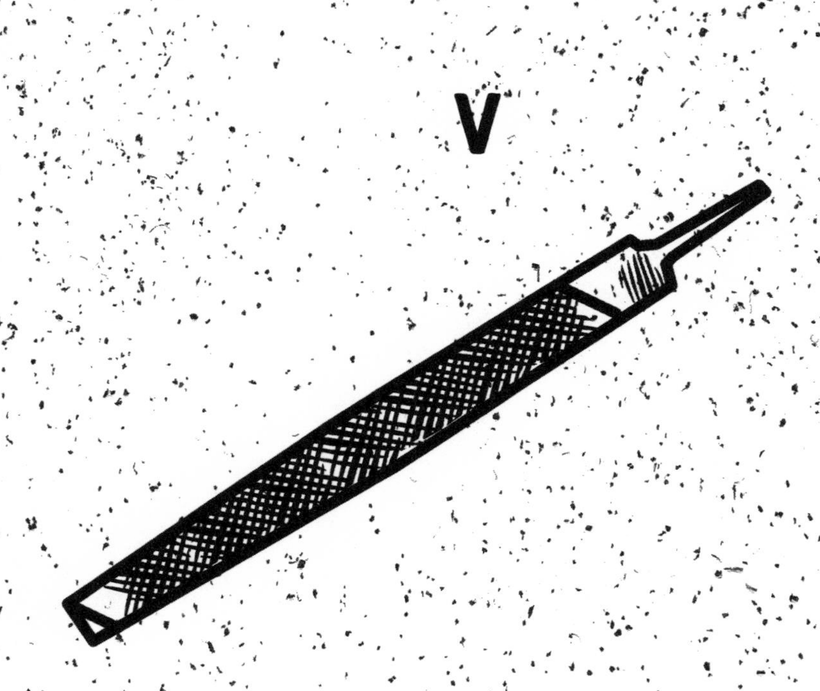

LOCKWOOD AVENUE

When it is lonely here in Grand Rapids and those wildernesses seem so much farther than beyond the 100th Meridian, I pace the confines of this house until I end in my living-room closet, flipping through twelve-year-old photo albums. I almost knead earthen images into duffy peninsula soil or St. Helens ash-dirt. Leaning closer toward snapshots, I feel wet winds sloughing off. Instead of closet walls, a blanket of devil's club. Instead of hardwood floors, towering false cedars. Fingers on photos, I realize if I had Pulaski-ed this world, there would be no straight-shot highways, no 9-to-5s, no subdivisions assembly-lined into broken images of Abraham Levitt and Sons©. I set down photos and stumble into a nightfall of mortgaged houses, bury face into this yard's only tree, then low into dirt's reek.

QUITTING

After six years given to trails, to crews,
this body wept for rest, mind frantic
for solitude, heart desperate for more
than glances of a woman through van
windows. One cannot fall in love through
windshields. After centuries of days calling
tent home, I silently waxed logger boots
a final time, threw leather gloves into trash,
transitioned into grad school, now this
professorship. But after four years of city
living, I find no love through house windows.

LOGGERS

No matter the times my fingers massage in beeswax, the spine remains crooked. Leather, stiff from working mountain creeks. Heels sloped from hiking hillsides and rock-strewn trails. These Westcoes gouged from the bite of an axe dinging into toe box. I have no reason to wear these boots. Still, they fit as if I commute each morning via trail rather than in a Honda Civic, listening to NPR news, worrying over lesson plans and the recession.

DESTINATIONS ON A MAP

These names are a song sung during lonely nights
after teaching at an urban university.

Icicle Creek, Whiskey Creek,
my troubles washed away in Troublesome Creek.

As streetlights burn through bedroom windows, washing
star myths from the sky, I sing this chorus.

Cascade Mountains, Disappointment Mountain,
we found grandeur camped on Glory Mountain.

I recite this hymn while idling at another red light
on the straight-line commute to work.

Buckhorn Lake, Image Lake,
we discovered our essence on Spirit Lake.

My voice rises until I am not here, but there,
until I am only mountain melody and creek chant.

MISSED

Sandstone-rough hands. A summer's
history in every nick, scab, scar.
Forest Service maps. An honest day.
An almost-empty tin of Obenhauf's
boot grease. False silence of night—
an owl caterwauling, the rustle
of a thermal through creekside willows.
A Pulaski adz to remove a Dutch
oven's iron lid. Sirius jumping on Shilo's
back, Red jumping on Sirius's back,
wide forest smiles. Evening beside
an April fire, Strings strumming
a five-string song to our Rogue owls.

NIGHT HOUSE

The house locked.
The hushed rays
of streetlights
blanketing
cabinets. A night
wind rattling
windowpanes.
Oak branches
banging against
siding. As if it—
the tree, the winds,
nightfall, all of it
—is calling.

GLORY GUARD STATION

Years after sculpting trail through wilderness,
        after crew scattered like seed,
        I return to trails and mountains
        as a writer-in-residence.

When these mountains last cradled me,
        that crew, and the later
        crews over the next five years,
        served as family.

Strangely, I return as professor gazing upon
        hands pale as a moon, soft as if
        they've never loved a tool
        other than a damned computer
mouse, never ripped steel heads into soil.

THINGS I NOTICE WHILE HIKING A TRAIL WE BUILT

A bleached elk femur, the white of death and decay, dead
three winters.
The club-shaped bone rests heavy in my hand—a memory
held tightly.

LOST LOVE

There is no love like
two arms loving
the hickory handle
of a McLeod, how
the hands know
exactly how to grasp
the shaft (though these
professorial hands
blister after moments).
The back knows just
how to curve, knees, too,
fall into their bend.
The body understands
its position, understands
how the rake chatters
across rock or, flipped,
how it pulls clods of
dirt. Even with a dozen
years of distance, our
bodies forget nothing.

THINGS I NOTICE WHILE HIKING A TRAIL WE BUILT

An evening primrose with heart-shaped petals glows
white in morning.
This flower is a solitary thing, a quiet and gentle thing,
as was life.

BASTARD

Those evenings, metal sang against metal as a bastard file ran toe to heel across our Pulaski's bit, removing its workday history—every rock nicked, mineral dirt thrown, spruce cleaved. Each trail scar disappearing as the bastard sheened its sharpening edge, clouding a cascade of steel. If twelve years ago I had cupped these hands and caught that metal rain, could there have been a way?

THINGS I NOTICE WHILE HIKING A TRAIL WE BUILT

A water bar Shilo and I installed, filled now with silt—
the cloggings of life.
If I carried a hog hoe, I'd return it to its flow, but
nothing stops time.

RETURN TO PRIMITIVE

After a week of writing these very trail poems, it's time
to leave these Glacier Peaks.

I cooler food, fold sheets, sweep the kitchen floor until
this cabin swims in dust and sunlight and

soon it's as if I've never spent a night in this log bunk,
never wandered these tangled woods.

When the cabin's interior is cleaned, lastly, I store
Pulaski and McLeod.

As I set trail tools aside—wishing I had brought a file
to sharpen their dulled edges—I notice,

not for the first time, that these soft artist fingers
have grown calloused

from holding the burled belly and throat of the Pulaski's
handle.

In one week it all returned, except those crew members.
I have nearly returned to primitive.

SHUTTER

I shutter the cabin and climb into my pickup.
        Today I dream this F-150 into a dinged-up
        white van, tool-heavy and crew-loaded.
But these early-morning hopes are ghosts.

I grind the truck into first and within moments,
        as a gentle blessing or a final good-bye,
Glory Peak offers itself to today's bruise-blue dawn.

I wave a lonely hand out an open window.
        To whom? Maybe to brother Shilo.
        Maybe to all the others, each lost to me
these last years. Maybe, simply, to Glory.

The view behind too soon obscured by
        whirling road-dust, a rising haze
stealing every image of Glory Peak.

It must be dust, I tell myself—not memory
        or that river of tears flowing like
        Agnes Creek—that prevents me
from seeing anything behind me at all.

Glossary of Trail Terms

Adz. An axe-like tool used for either planing logs or digging into dirt.

Backcountry. A remote location, normally in a wilderness setting, often without roads or structures.

Bar Oil. Oil that lubricates the chain and bar on a chainsaw.

Bastard File. A coarse-cut file used to sharpen blades of woods tools, often the Pulaski axe-head.

Brush. Plants, bushes, and tree branches. "To brush" means to clear brush from beside a trail.

Bull of the Woods. The leader of a woods operation.

Crew Leader. The leader of a crew of trail builders for the Northwest Youth Corps.

Crew Members. Youth who hire on to Northwest Youth Corps to work during spring, summer, and fall. Normally between sixteen and nineteen years old. Crew members are paid hourly to build trails.

Crosscut Saw. A two-person handsaw designed for bucking and felling trees. Used, since it has no engine, in Wilderness areas.

Cut Bank. The angled wall on the uphill side after a trail has been cut into earth.

Cutters. The part of the chainsaw chain's teeth that cuts into trees.

DBH. Short for "diameter at breast height." A way of measuring the thickness of a tree.

Dead and Down. Any dead tree lying upon the earth.

Dogs. Spikes mounted where the chainsaw bar connects to the power head. Chainsaw dogs, when jammed into a log, function as a fulcrum for swinging the bar and chain through the tree being sawed.

Duff. Decaying organic plant matter (including leaves, needles, plants, and grasses).

Dutch Oven. A cast-iron cooking pot with a tight-fitting lid. In the backcountry a Dutch oven is surrounded on all sides with hot coals and used like an oven. Also known as a Dutchie.

Ear Pro. Short for ear protection. Used while chainsawing to protect hearing.

Eye Pro. Short for eye protection. Used while chainsawing to protect eyesight from flying debris.

Gorp. Short for "good old raisins and peanuts." A snack often eaten in the woods.

Grub. A verb meaning "to dig."

Hickory Shirt. A strong twilled-cotton shirt. Has vertical stripes and a zipper near the collar. Used as a work shirt, especially for chainsawing, since the zipper keeps wood chips from going into the collar.

High Reach Saw. A handsaw with a telescopic pole for reaching high limbs in a tree.

Hitch. The term used for going into the backcountry for at least one overnight, but often for much longer. Also known as spike.

Hazel Hoe. A heavy-duty type of hoe, with a grubbing blade on one side and a sledgehammer face on the other. Good for both digging and light sledgehammer work.

Heartwood. The oldest, densest, darkest wood in a tree. The center wood of the tree.

Hog Hoe. Also known as a grub hoe. A medium-duty hoe with a thin grubbing blade. Great for digging into soil. Easily damaged.

Logger Boots. Thick leather boots designed for logging, normally at least ten inches high and possessing both a logger heal and a logger tongue.

Loowit. The Klickitat name for Mount St. Helens.

Loppers. A cutting tool, used especially for pruning trees and brush.

Mattock. A heavy-duty, two-part tool. One side is a pick used for digging in rocky soil. The other side is an adz for digging in dirt. Also known as a pick-adz.

McLeod. A long-handled, two-sided tool. One side has an oversized hoe used for digging. The other side has tines for removing brush and rocks from trails.

Northwest Youth Corps. Also known as NYC. This nonprofit, created in 1984, offers youth an education-based work experience modeled on the 1930s Civilian Conservation Corps. NYC serves over one thousand youth in Oregon, Washington, northern California, and Idaho a year.

Oly or Olympia. A type of beer named after the Olympic Mountains.

Pick-adz. See mattock.

Pulaski. A two-part tool. One side possesses an axe and the other side an adz. Great for cutting through trees and digging in dirt.

Rainer. A type of beer named after Mount Rainer.

Rakers. The part of the chainsaw chain that cleans sawed material from the logs so the cutters can continue to cut.

Rock Bar. A four-foot-long, heavy (15–20 lbs.) metal bar used for prying up boulders.

Slash. Branches left behind after cutting down a tree. When piled, it is known as a slash pile.

Spike. See hitch.

Stihl. A chainsaw known for its orange-and-white paint job.

Tool Count. The call given ("Tool count!") before taking a break or finishing for the day. During tool count all tools are brought together and counted to ensure no tools have been left in the brush.

Westco Logger Boots. Short for West Coast Logger Boots. An Oregon-based shoe company that specializes in logger boots.

Wilderness. Land that has been federally designated as Wilderness (from the Wilderness Act of 1964) prohibits the use of engines, gears, and machines. Only foot and horse traffic are allowed.

wilderness. From the term "self-willed lands." Wild, undeveloped, and primordial land.

Acknowledgments

The following poems were previously published in these journals, sometimes in slightly different form:

About Place: "Wilderness Language"
AMP: "Beard"
Artemis: "Destinations on a Map"
Camas: The Nature of the West: "Hands & Fingers"
Cirque: "Driving Late at Night, the Crew Asleep, Many Miles Left to Travel" and "Prospect"
Cream City Review: "Desolation Nights," "Love Song," "Rain along Whiskey Creek," and "Why am I yelling? I'll tell you why"
Eastern Iowa Review: "Nouns of Assembly"
Green Mountains Review: "Hitch" and "Stripping"
The Hopper: "Savage Quitting"
Kudzu House Quarterly: "Distance"
Mud Season Review: "Morning Freedom"
Orson's Review: "After a Ten-Hour Day," "Autumn's Outfit," "Entropy," "Retreat," "Gospel," and "Wild Cacophony"
Pilgrimage Magazine: "Hickory" and "Lost Love"
Southern Humanities Review: "Dismemberment of a Stihl Chainsaw"
Superstition Review: "Pull" and "Rain Gear"
Turtle Island Quarterly: "Logger Boots"
Under the Sun Literary Magazine: "Bastard," "Enough," and "What I Learn about the City during the Pause between Dusk & Dark"
Uproot: "Glory Guard Station," "Loggers," "Nowhere Road," "Tomorrow," "Shutter," and "Trail Crew"
Windfall: "In the Days after Our Breakup"

All artwork was created by and is used courtesy of Tim Calkins.

Crosscut: Poems was written with financial support from Norwich University and with support from the San Juan National Forest.